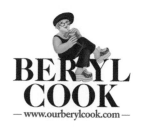

BERYL COOK
— www.ourberylcook.com —

NAKED TRUTH
JOURNAL

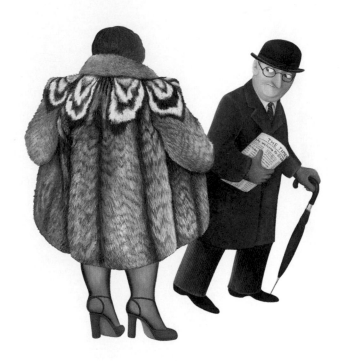

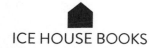

ICE HOUSE BOOKS

Published by Ice House Books

© 2019 John Cook. Licensed by Iris.
www.thisisiris.co.uk
www.berylcook.com

Illustrations by Beryl Cook

Written by Rebecca Du Pontet & Designed by Emily Curtis

Ice House Books is an imprint of Half Moon Bay Limited
The Ice House, 124 Walcot Street, Bath, BA1 5BG
www.icehousebooks.co.uk

ISBN 978-1-912867-45-5

Printed in China

This Journal Belongs To

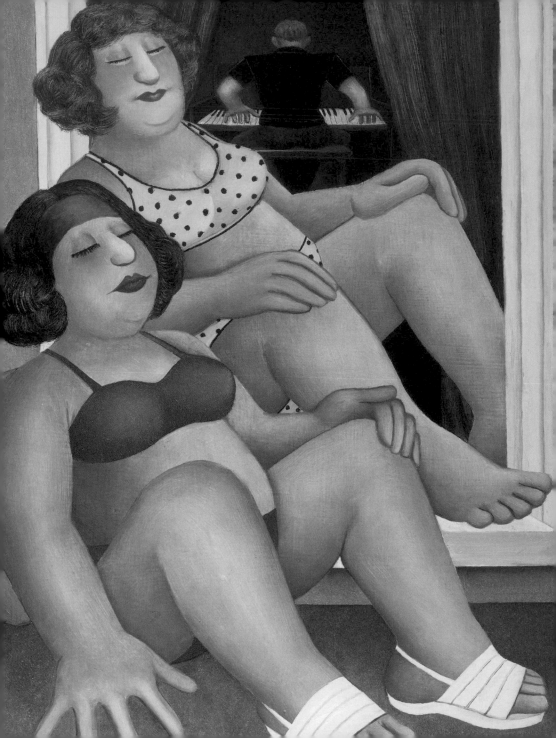

Share your naked truths . . .

Reasons to be Cheerful

Date:

Date:

Date:

Reasons to be Cheerful

Date:

Date:

Date:

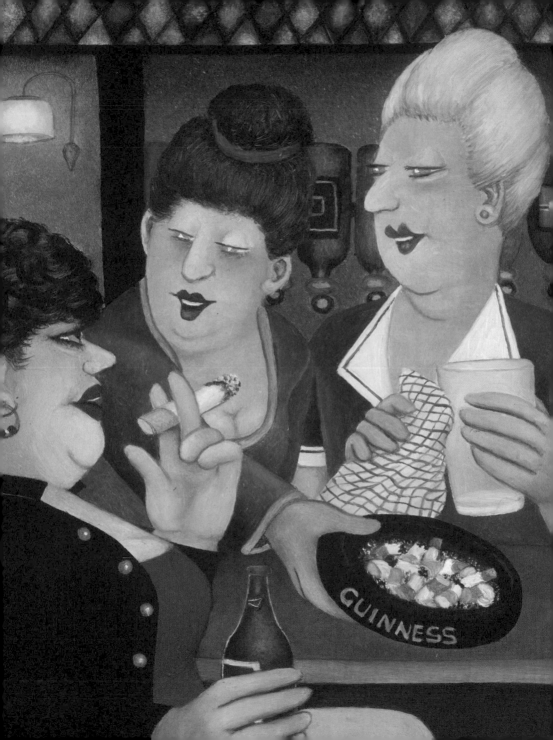

A problem shared is a problem halved.

Reasons to be Cheerful

Date:

Date:

Date:

Reasons to be Cheerful

Date:

Date:

Date:

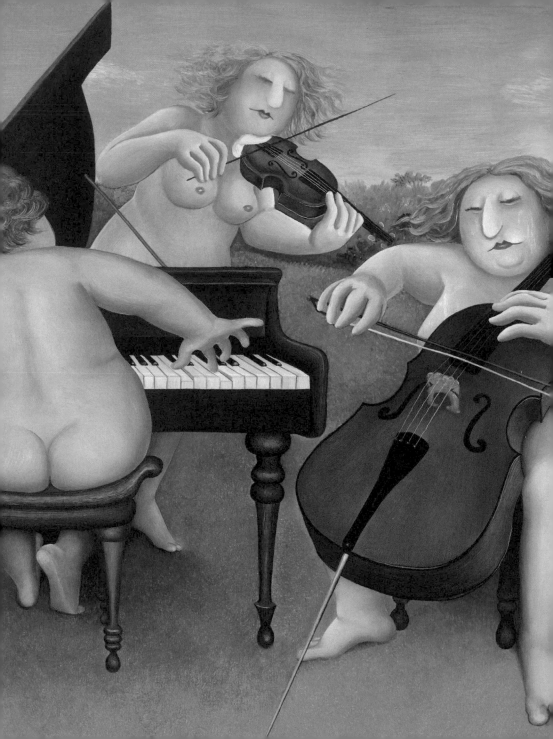

Rejoice in your talents!

Reasons to be Cheerful

Date:

Date:

Date:

Reasons to be Cheerful

Date:

Date:

Date:

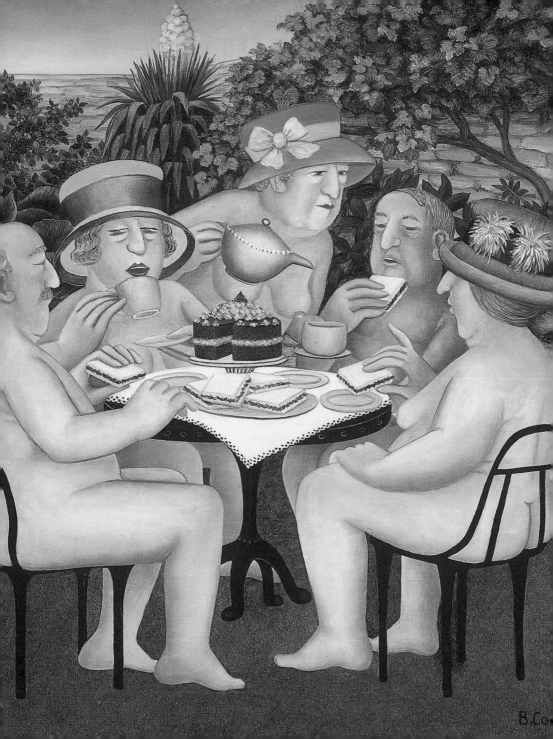

Time spent with friends is never wasted.

Reasons to be Cheerful

Date:

Date:

Date:

Reasons to be Cheerful

Date:

Date:

Date:

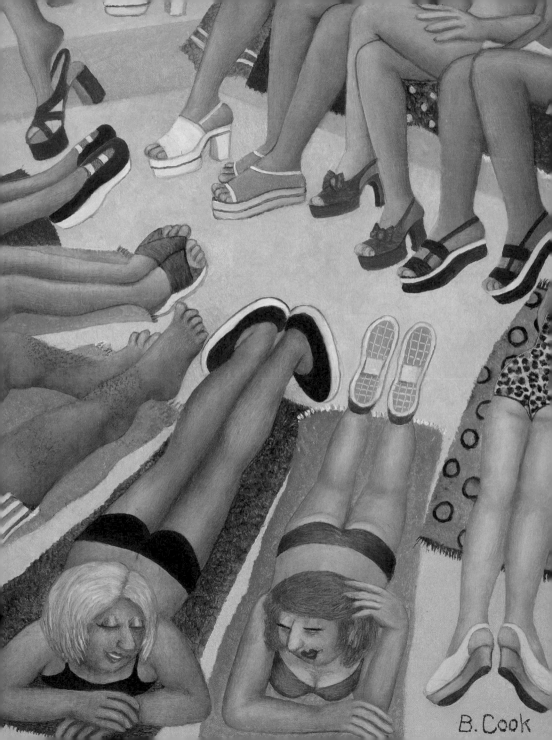

B. Cook

Don't sweat the small stuff.

Reasons to be Cheerful

Date:

Date:

Date:

Reasons to be Cheerful

Date:

Date:

Date:

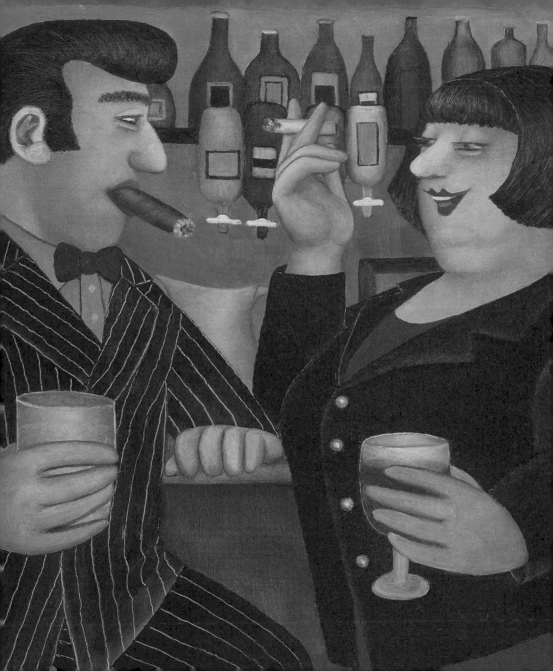

Make time for important hobbies.

Reasons to be Cheerful

Date:

Date:

Date:

Reasons to be Cheerful

Date:

Date:

Date:

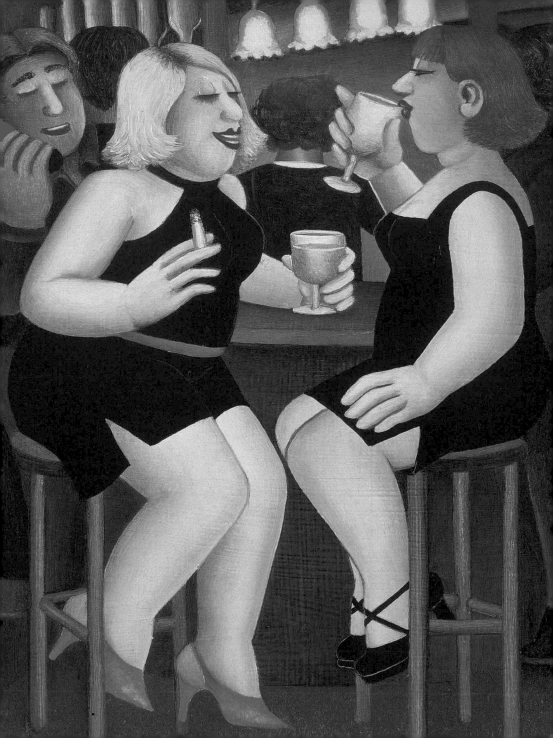

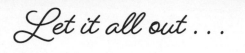
Let it all out . . .

Reasons to be Cheerful

Date:

Date:

Date:

Reasons to be Cheerful

Date:

Date:

Date:

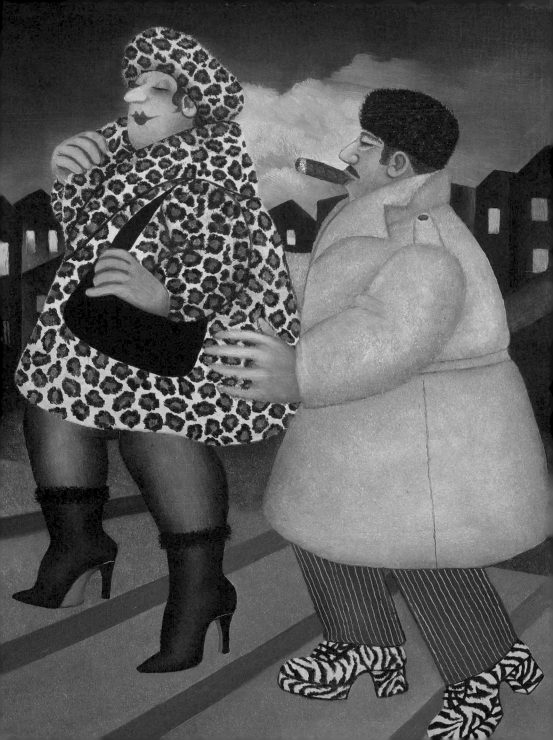

Don't be afraid to stand out.

Reasons to be Cheerful

Date:

Date:

Date:

Reasons to be Cheerful

Date:

Date:

Date:

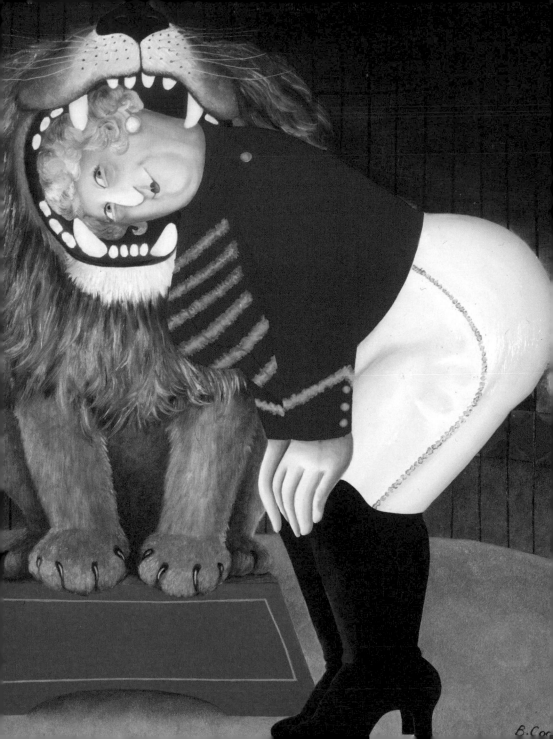

Do something daring today!

Reasons to be Cheerful

Date:

Date:

Date:

Reasons to be Cheerful

Date:

Date:

Date:

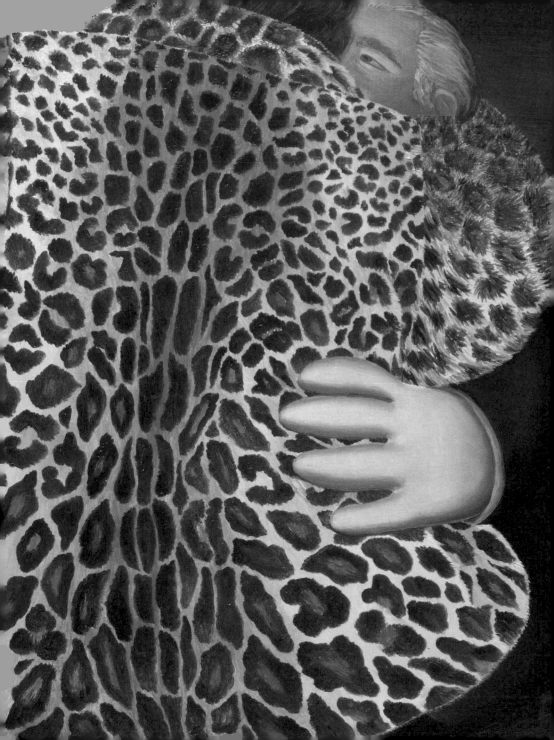

The best things in life are free . . .

Reasons to be Cheerful

Date:

Date:

Date:

Reasons to be Cheerful

Date:

Date:

Date:

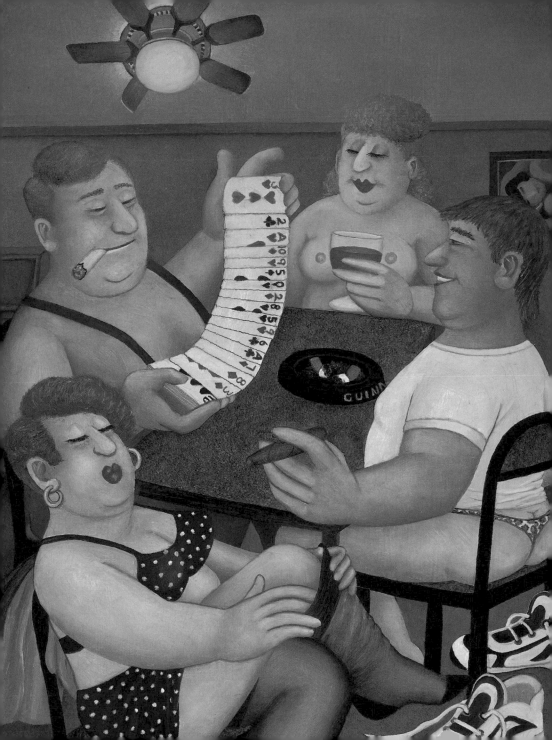

Keep your cards close to your chest.

Reasons to be Cheerful

Date:

Date:

Date:

Reasons to be Cheerful

Date:

Date:

Date:

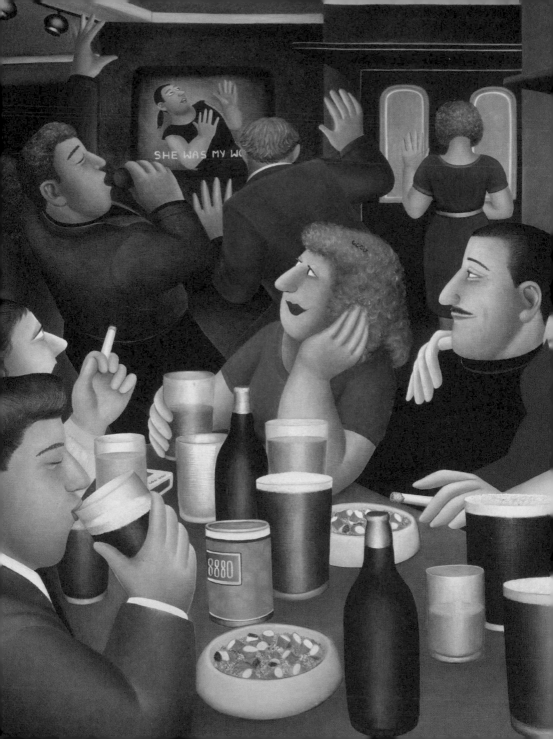

Life is what you make it.

Reasons to be Cheerful

Date:

Date:

Date:

Reasons to be Cheerful

Date:

Date:

Date:

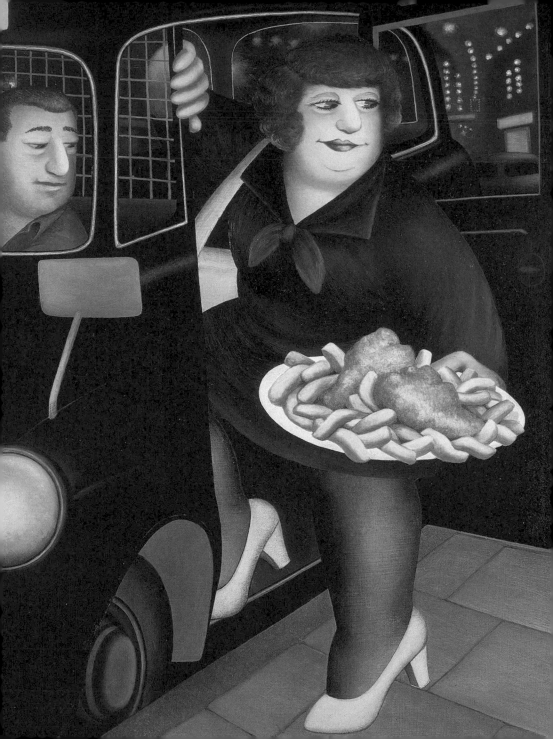

Allow yourself occasional indulgences.

Reasons to be Cheerful

Date:

Date:

Date:

Reasons to be Cheerful

Date:

Date:

Date:

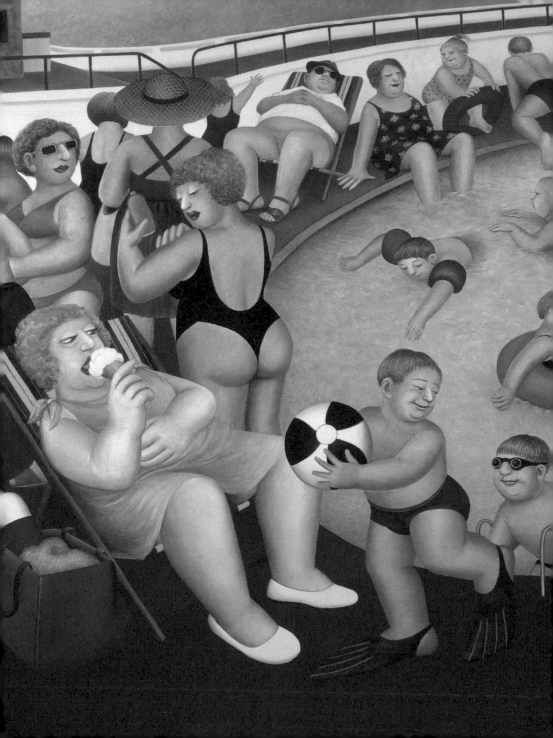

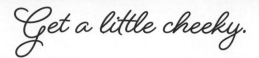

Get a little cheeky.

Reasons to be Cheerful

Date:

Date:

Date:

Reasons to be Cheerful

Date:

Date:

Date:

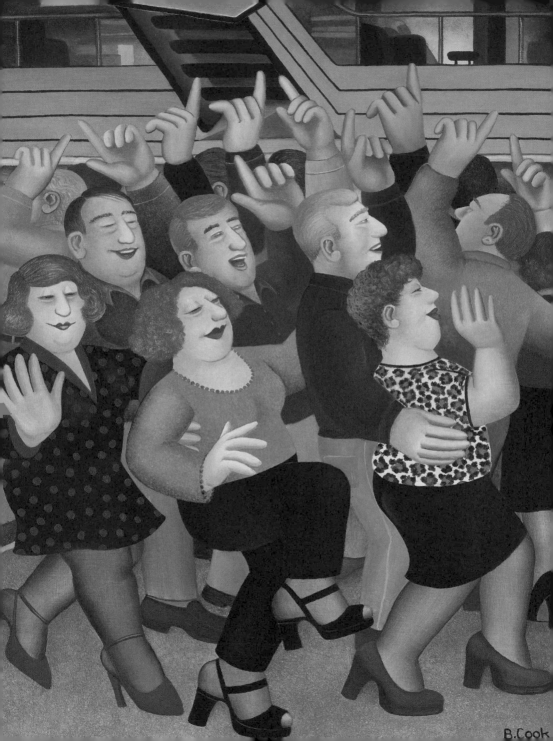

Make the most of every day!

Reasons to be Cheerful

Date:

Date:

Date:

Reasons to be Cheerful

Date:

Date:

Date:

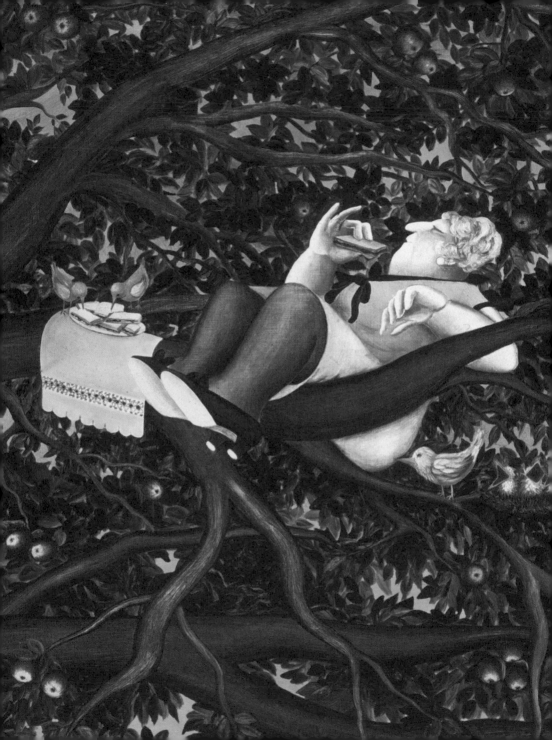

Find your happy place.